# The Magic School Bus
## PRESENTS
### Sea Creatures

Scholastic Inc.

*Previous page:* A great white shark

Photos © 2014: Alamy Images: 12 inset (Beverly Factor), 21 left (Johnny Johnson), 30 (Kip Evans), 29 top left (Norbert Probst), 28 top left (Reinhard Dirscherl), 8 bottom right (Stephen Frink), 17 center (WaterFrame); Getty Images: 22 bottom right, 25 right (David Fleetham), 9 (Franco Banfi), 3 (Mark Carwardine), 25 left (Reinhard Dirscherl); iStockphoto: cover Angel Fish (DJMattaar), cover background (stephankhofs); Nature Picture Library: 21 right, 23, 24 (Alex Mustard), 1 (Constantinos Petrinos), 12 background, 13 (David Fleetham), 6 top, 27 bottom left (David Shale), 6 inset bottom (Doc White), 11 top, 11 bottom left, 22 top (Doug Perrine), 18 left (Georgette Douwma), 29 top right (Ingo Arndt), 4 inset, 14 left, 28 bottom left (Jurgen Freund), 16 (Lundgren), 22 bottom left (Nuno Sa), 29 bottom left (Todd Mintz), 3 bottom and 20 (Troels Jacobsen/Arcticphoto), 6 background, 7 (Wild Wonders of Europe/ Lundgren); NOAA: 26 left, 27 bottom right, 27 center (Dr. Bob Embley, NOAA PMEL, Chief Scientist), 26 right (Okeanos Explorer Program, Galapagos Rift Expedition 2011); Science Photo Library: 17 right (Alexander Semenov), 8 top (Louise Murray), 15 (Peter Scoones), 27 top (Phillipe Crassous), 28 bottom right (Scubazoo); Science Source: 31 left (Alexis Rosenfeld), 31 right (F.S. Westmoreland), 18 inset right (Frans Lanting); Shutterstock, Inc.: cover turtle (dive-hive), 18 background, 19 (Ethan Daniels), 29 bottom right (Greg Amptman), 28 top right (Krzysztof Odziomek), 10 (Mogens Trolle), 17 left (Nicolas Aznavour), 3 bottom and 8 bottom left (Studio 37), 4 background, 5 (Susan McKenzie); Superstock, Inc./NaturePL: 3 center and 14 right.

ISBN 978-0-545-68366-1

Produced by Potomac Global Media, LLC

Published by Scholastic Inc., 557 Broadway, New York, NY 10012.

14 13 12                                                                                     20 21 22/0

Cover design by Paul Banks
Interior design by Carol Farrar Norton

Printed in the U.S.A.     40
First printing, July 2014

# Contents

p. 8

p. 14

p. 20

# At the Beach

**T**oday, we are going to learn about sea creatures," said Ms. Frizzle, "and what better place to start than at the beach?" The beach is where the land meets the sea, with the rise and fall of the tide. The seawater is shallow here. Many animals visit the seashore, including seals, seabirds, and crabs.

These red crabs live on land in forests. But they come back to the beach every year to lay their eggs in the water.

The tide rises and falls twice a day along most coastlines.

I SEE THE SEA

## Seaweed
Seaweed is thickest near the shore. It grows in shallow water, where there is plenty of light.

That's a lot of water!!

## World oceans
by Carlos

The ocean covers nearly three-quarters of the world. All that salt water is connected in one giant sea, but we name its different parts. The five major parts are the Atlantic, the Arctic, the Indian, the Pacific, and the Southern Oceans. The largest of them all is the Pacific Ocean, which lies to the west of the United States. At 63.8 million square miles (165.25 million square kilometers), the Pacific Ocean is bigger than all the land on Earth put together.

## Seals
**Seals are good swimmers. They come ashore to rest and give birth to pups.**

## Frizzle Fact
**The length of all the world's coastlines measures around the same distance as a journey to the Moon (217,500 miles/350,000 kilometers).**

# Open Water

This crustacean (an amphipod) is a plankton. Amphipods are usually smaller than your thumbnail.

**A**way from the shore, the ocean is full of plankton of all sizes. Plankton is the name given to any plant or animal that cannot swim against a current. It just floats in the water. Plankton includes algae, crustaceans, and jellyfish such as the Portuguese man-of-war. Most plankton is too small to be seen with the naked eye.

## Sting in the tail
Tentacles lined with venomous stingers trail 30 feet (9 meters) behind the Portuguese man-of-war.

## Tangled trap
Fish get trapped in the tentacles and are stung to death before being hauled up to the body and eaten.

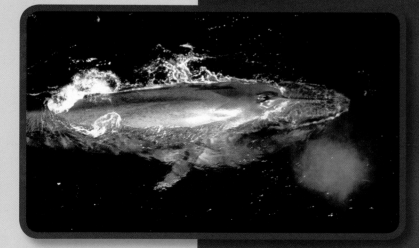

Blue whales are the largest animals in the world — three times the size of a school bus.

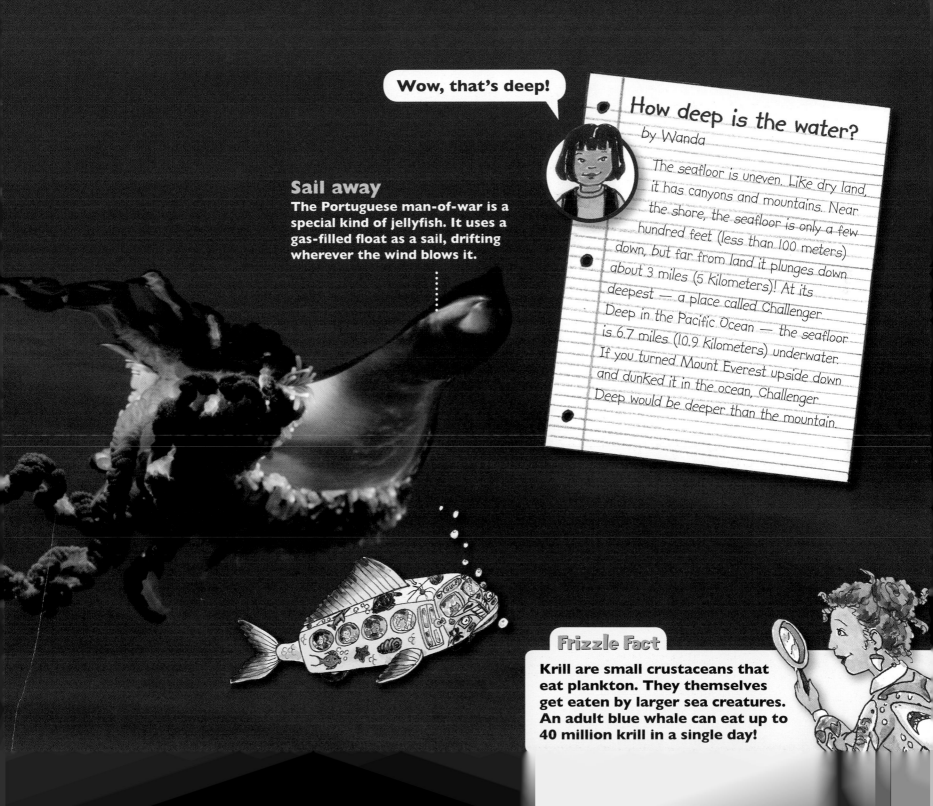

**Wow, that's deep!**

## How deep is the water?
by Wanda

The seafloor is uneven. Like dry land, it has canyons and mountains. Near the shore, the seafloor is only a few hundred feet (less than 100 meters) down, but far from land it plunges down about 3 miles (5 kilometers)! At its deepest — a place called Challenger Deep in the Pacific Ocean — the seafloor is 6.7 miles (10.9 kilometers) underwater. If you turned Mount Everest upside down and dunked it in the ocean, Challenger Deep would be deeper than the mountain.

### Sail away
**The Portuguese man-of-war is a special kind of jellyfish. It uses a gas-filled float as a sail, drifting wherever the wind blows it.**

### Frizzle Fact
**Krill are small crustaceans that eat plankton. They themselves get eaten by larger sea creatures. An adult blue whale can eat up to 40 million krill in a single day!**

Some tuna can weigh up to 775 pounds (350 kilograms). That's as much as a motorcycle!

# Fish

There are thousands of different types of fish in the sea. They all have a skeleton and a skull like humans, but they don't have any arms or legs, only fins. A fish's body is often sleek and smooth so it can cut through the water.

Seahorses suck up tiny sea creatures using their tube-shaped snouts.

**Frizzle Fact**

Seahorse dads are special. They take the mom's eggs into a pouch and later give birth to their babies.

These long, slender fish called ribbon eels live coiled up under rocks. They only slip out to snap up a small fish or two.

**Sunfish**
Sunfish feed on small fish, jellyfish, and mollusks.

I ♥ gills!

## Why don't fish drown?
by Phoebe

Fish don't breathe air the way we do. Instead, they take oxygen from the water using their gills.

The water goes in through the mouth and runs over the gills, which are behind the head on both sides. The gills are full of blood, which absorbs the oxygen from the water. The water then flows out of the gill slits on the sides of the fish's body.

oxygen dissolved in water

water

gills take in oxygen

water

water passes through

The ocean sunfish is almost round and looks like a giant head with just a tail. It can grow as big as a tractor tire.

A sunfish can lay 300 million eggs a year.

# Sharks!

The great white shark is the world's biggest hunting fish. It attacks seals that swim at the surface of the ocean.

**M**any sharks, including hammerheads and great whites, are powerful hunting fish with sharp teeth. They use super senses to track their prey. Sharks swim by swishing their big tails from side to side. Thick fins keep them going in a straight line.

A hammerhead shark's head acts like a satellite dish. It helps the shark's electric sensors detect prey.

# Shark Super Senses

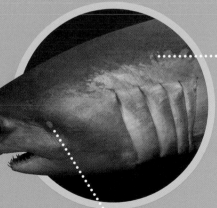

### Electric sensor
Sensors in a shark's snout pick up electricity coming from other animals — even ones buried in sand.

### Motion sensor
Motion sensors run along the side of the body and pick up the water ripples made by fish swimming nearby, which is very useful in the dark!

### Nose
Nostrils in the snout are used for smelling. A shark can detect a single drop of blood in one million drops of water.

### Ear
A tiny ear behind each eye can pick up splashing sounds from up to one mile (1.6 kilometers) away.

Sharp teeth ahoy!

### Why are a shark's teeth so sharp?
by Ralphie

A great white shark's teeth have pointed tips, like arrowheads, that cut right into whatever they bite. The sides of the teeth are jagged, like the cutting edge of a saw. This makes them even better at slicing. The teeth fall out very easily, but new ones grow to replace them. A great white shark can go through 3,000 teeth in its lifetime!

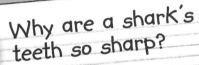
Great white shark teeth 1¼–2 inches (3–5 centimeters)

# At the Coral Reef

**C**orals look like oddly shaped, colorful plants and rocks. In fact, they are made up of tiny animals. Coral reefs are home to many other sea creatures, including turtles, fish, sea stars, sharks, and even snakes!

One-quarter of all sea creatures — including this sea star — live on or around coral reefs.

### Frizzle Fact
**The Great Barrier Reef in Australia is 1,600 miles (2,575 kilometers) long. It would cover half of Texas.**

### Green sea turtle
Green sea turtles look for clumps of seaweed to chomp on.

**Butterfly fish**
As brightly colored as any butterfly, these fish use their pointed snouts to nibble on corals when feeding.

**Polyp city!**

## What are corals made of?
by Tim

A lump of coral is made up of thousands of individual creatures called polyps. A polyp is like a tiny upside-down jellyfish with a hard but very thin shell. When polyps die, they leave their empty shells behind and a new set of polyps grows on top. Very slowly — over hundreds of years — the layers of shell build up and grow into rocky lumps made from billions of polyp skeletons. Only the surface is alive, but don't touch! Dead polyps are hard as rock, but living ones are fragile.

**School's out**
To stay safe, smaller fish swim in groups called schools.

# Underwater Reptiles

The tail of a sea snake is a flattened paddle, which helps it swim underwater.

Reptiles are animals with scaly skin. They include snakes, turtles, crocodiles, and lizards. While most reptiles live on land, some of the largest are found in the sea. They all have lungs, so sea reptiles have to surface every now and then to take a breath of fresh air.

Green sea turtles feed on crabs and jellyfish when they are young. As adults, they eat sea grasses and algae.

## Frizzle Fact

Most sea reptiles go back onto land to lay their eggs. The shells of their eggs are not waterproof.

A turtle can hold its breath for about 20 minutes when it is swimming underwater.

**Down it goes!**

### How leatherbacks eat jellyfish
by Dorothy Ann

Leatherback turtles feed on jellyfish. These animals are very slippery, and would slither back out of a turtle's throat if the leatherback did not have a special trap. The turtle's throat is covered in hooked spikes that snag onto the jellyfish. It means the jellies cannot drift back up the throat — they can only go down into the turtle's stomach.

**Marine iguanas sunbathe on rocks to get warm before diving into the cold seawater to eat seaweed.**

There is only one lizard that likes the sea — the marine iguana. It lives on just a few Pacific islands.

**Hi, cousin!**

# Shellfish

**Walk like a crab**
Like this brown crab, many crabs walk sideways to get from place to place.

Look, I'm a hermit crab! These crabs don't grow shells, but move into empty ones they find on the seafloor.

Great! I found one that fits!

**M**any common sea creatures are types of shellfish. Their soft bodies are protected inside a hard outer shell. Crabs, lobsters, and other shellfish with legs are called crustaceans. The most common shellfish are mollusks. You can find their shells washed up on the beach. Mollusks include sea snails, clams, mussels, and scallops.

**Pearls of wisdom!**

### How do pearls grow?
by Ralphie

Shiny, smooth pearls form inside the shells of shellfish, such as oysters. The insides of these shells are coated with a shimmering blue-green substance called mother-of-pearl. Any speck of sand trapped inside the shell gets coated, too. Over many years (and many coats) the sand grows into a beautiful pearl. The biggest pearl ever found was 9 inches (23 centimeters) across and came from the Philippines. If you wanted to buy it, it would cost about $40 million — the same price as a passenger jet.

The mantis shrimp has the sharpest eyes in the sea. Each eye has 10,000 lenses and can see heat and other rays that are invisible to humans.

A lobster has ten legs. The first two have huge pincers. These are used to snap at attackers and crack open other shellfish.

Many mollusks, such as these mussels, are filter feeders. They collect and eat plankton from the water.

# In the Kelp Forest

These spiky animals are sea urchins. They nibble away at the base of the thick kelp stems.

The kelp forest is another part of the ocean filled with life. A type of seaweed, kelp grows 12 stories tall. Little gas bags on its stalks keep it floating upright. Kelp forests are home to sea otters and slow-moving shellfish like sea urchins and sea stars.

Sea otters eat sea urchins and other shellfish that live on the seafloor below the kelp.

**Frizzle Fact**

Chemicals from kelp are used in medicines for upset stomachs.

The world's fastest-growing plant, giant kelp grows up to 2 feet (60 centimeters) in a day!

## Sea stars

Sea stars live in many ocean habitats. A sea star's mouth is on the underside of its body.

Sea otters crack me up!

How do sea otters crack shells?
by Arnold

A sea otter collects a shellfish from the seafloor. Once at the water's surface, the otter floats on its back, resting the shell on its chest. Then, using a stone kept tucked in its armpit, the sea otter hammers on the shell until it cracks open and the otter gets to eat the meat inside.

# Flippers and Whiskers

Blubber, the thick fat under the skin, helps seals and walruses stay afloat in the water.

## Toothy cousins

Walruses are relatives of seals that live near the North Pole. They use their tusks to haul themselves out of the water for a rest on floating ice.

## Frizzle Fact

A walrus has 6 inches (15 centimeters) of fatty blubber to keep it warm in icy water.

**H**umans are mammals. Mammals have hair and drink milk when they are babies. Seals, sea lions, and walruses are mammals, too, but they live in the sea. People sometimes confuse seals and sea lions. Sea lions stand up on four flippers and have ears that you can see, but seals have short flippers and lie on their tummies.

Who's eating whom?

### The ocean food chain
by Keesha

Seals and walruses are near the top of the ocean food chain. This chain starts with teeny floating plant plankton. These are eaten by tiny floating animal plankton, which are themselves eaten by larger animals like fish and mollusks. These are what seals and walruses eat — but there is always a bigger fish! Sharks are the ocean's top predators, along with killer whales and polar bears.

A harbor seal pup grows up fast. It learns to swim just a few hours after birth and starts hunting at the age of three weeks.

Seals use their whiskers to pick up the movements of fish and other prey in the water.

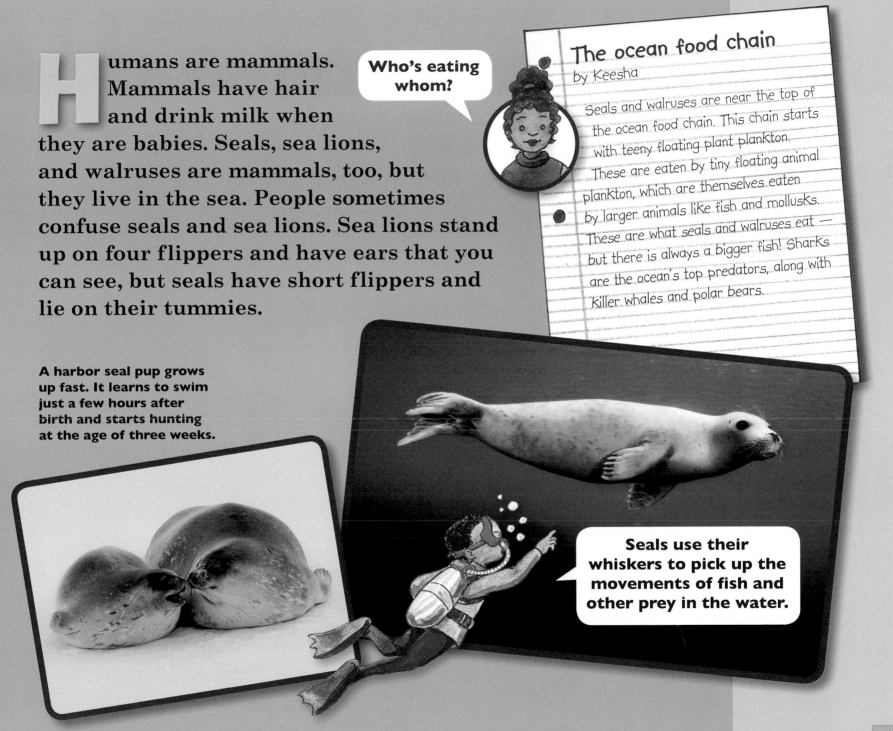

# Dolphins and Whales

**W**hales and dolphins look a lot like fish—they have fins and tails—but they are really mammals. They breathe air, but unlike seals, dolphins and whales never come onto land. Smooth skin is better than hair in water, so these sea mammals have just a few wisps of hair when they are young.

**Killer whales are actually large dolphins. They use their super-strong jaws to crush their prey.**

**A sperm whale calf swims with its mother. All dolphins and whales are born underwater.**

## Whale Survival

### Blowhole
Whales and dolphins have to surface for air. They use one, sometimes two, big nostrils on the top of the head to breathe.

### Sifting food
Most whales sift food from seawater using a sievelike curtain in the mouth, called baleen.

### Water spout
When whales breathe out, a spout of water droplets shoots up into the air.

## Bottlenose dolphin

Bottlenose dolphins live in groups called pods. They are always on the move, working together to find fish, crabs, or squid to eat.

Hey, let's listen in.

### Do dolphins talk?
by Wanda

Dolphins produce really high-pitched squeaks and clicks. Humans can't hear these sounds, but dolphins use them to find their way around underwater. The noises they make bounce off other things in the water, and the echo tells the dolphin where those things are. Dolphins also squawk and chirrup to one another and send messages by splashing.

A dolphin has no nose — it smells with its tongue instead!

# Jellies and Tentacles

## Beautiful but deadly

This blue-ringed octopus is only the size of a golf ball, but it has a very venomous bite. The blue rings are a warning to stay away.

The only hard part of an octopus is a sharp beak hidden at the base of its eight tentacles.

Venom is a poison. It can be deadly.

**T**entacles are used by both the simplest and the smartest sea creatures. A jellyfish is very simple. It grabs prey with its tentacles and hauls it up to its bag-shaped body. Squids and octopuses have tentacles, too. They are good hunters with big brains and eyes for spotting prey. . . and each other.

# Tubes and Tentacles

## Jet propulsion

Squids are jet-powered; they squirt water through a flexible tube to push themselves in any direction.

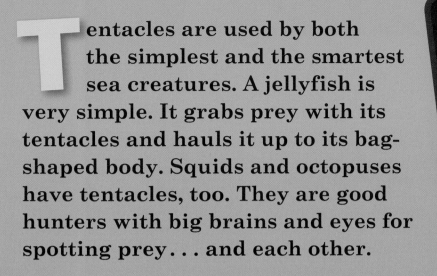

## Mean tentacles

A squid's tentacles have suckers for grabbing prey and pulling them toward the mouth.

Some jellyfish can make their bodies glow and flash in the dark. The lights confuse and deter predators.

I spy with my big eye!

### How giant is a giant squid?
by Tim

The giant squid grows to an average length of 33 feet (10 meters), including tentacles. That's about ten times longer than me. They have been known to reach twice this size. A giant squid's eyes can be as big as 10 inches (25 centimeters) across — that's about the size of a pizza. Little light reaches the deep sea, where giant squids live. Having such big eyes helps them spot their prey.

# In the Vent World

A hydrothermal vent is also called a smoker because the water becomes cloudy when it mixes with the rest of the ocean.

**F**inally the bus reached the seabed, where the toughest sea creatures live. We saw a hydrothermal vent — super-hot water coming from within the Earth. The Friz explained, "The water is full of volcanic chemicals that only bacteria can eat. Time to leave, before the weight of this deep water crushes our bus!"

It's too dark to see anything down here, but we can use our headlights!

**Tube worm**
Bacteria grow inside these giant worms. They provide a steady supply of nutrients.

**Frizzle Fact**
Scientists think that the first life may have evolved in vents.

## Hot worm

Close up, a bristle worm looks like an alien!

## Mussels

These mussels sift bacteria from the hot water around the vent.

**We're in hot water!**

## How does a vent work?
by Carlos

A hydrothermal vent is a little like a spring on dry land. Seawater trickles through cracks in the seafloor and gathers hundreds of feet (several hundred meters) below. The rocks are very hot down there, but the sheer weight of the ocean keeps the water from boiling away. Instead, it rushes back to the seafloor, where it gushes out in the form of a smoker.

## Ghost lobster

This pale lobster snips bits off tube worms to eat. It can live in hot, poisonous water.

## Spiky snapper

This spiny crab scuttles around, snapping up whatever prey it finds. It is protected from predators by spiky armor.

# Our Favorite Sea Creatures!

## Sailfish

This is one of the fastest fish in the sea. It can zoom through the water at 65 miles (105 kilometers) per hour! Sailfish use speed to stun their prey. They hit them with their pointed snouts! The fish only raises its sail-like fin when it wants to look bigger — or scare off predators.

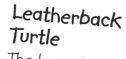

## Whale Shark

The whale shark is the biggest fish in the sea. It is 40 feet (12 meters) long and has a mouth that is 5 feet (1.5 meters) wide. Although this creature is a shark, it does not attack prey. Instead, it swims along with its big mouth wide open and sifts plankton from the water.

## Horseshoe Crab

We call this creature a crab, but it's really a prehistoric underwater bug! It has ten legs and crawls along the seafloor catching worms. If it gets knocked onto its back, it flips upright using its spiky tail. Weirdest of all, this bug has blue blood.

## Leatherback Turtle

The largest sea turtle is the leatherback. Instead of being hard, this turtle's shell is covered in a soft leathery skin. An adult turtle is a massive 7 feet (210 meters) long and 9 feet (240 meters) wide (including flippers). Leatherbacks live all over the ocean, except in the coldest parts.

## Giant Clam

This huge *bivalve* has the biggest shell in the world — it is more than 4 feet (1.2 meters) wide. A giant clam can live for 100 years or more, with a little help from some tiny plants called algae. These plants live inside the clam's brightly colored body and make sugar on which the clam can feed.

**Well done, class! I hope you can join me on our next adventure!**

## Sea Lion

Sea lions (and *seals*) that are born in the Arctic have white fur, which is handy when it comes to hiding from polar bears!  Sea lions are also known as fur seals because their hair is very shaggy. Look closely and you can also see their ears — seals don't have visible ears.

## Narwhal

The narwhal is the closest thing the world has to a unicorn. This strange whale lives in the Arctic and has 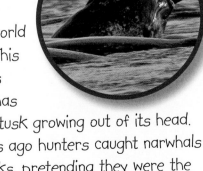 one long, spiraled tusk growing out of its head. Hundreds of years ago hunters caught narwhals and sold their tusks, pretending they were the magical horns of unicorns.

## Manatee

This unusual-looking marine mammal shares features with a *seal* or a dolphin, but is actually a type of sea cow. It lives  along coastlines, grazing on seaweed. However, the manatee is not related to cows. In fact, its closest relative is the elephant!

29

# Saving the Ocean

**S**ome of our garbage ends up in the ocean. This causes problems for the creatures living there. The chemicals in the garbage poison some animals that mistake it for food. Scientists say that in every patch of ocean the size of a football field, there are around 3,000 pieces of plastic trash. The entire ocean adds up to 72 billion football fields, so that's a lot of garbage.

## ⟨ Marine sanctuaries

The United States has fourteen marine sanctuaries — places where the seafloor (and the water above it) is protected by law. These sanctuaries include the coral reefs of the Florida Keys (opposite), the kelp forests of Monterey Bay, and whale feeding grounds at Stellwagen Bank off the coast of Massachusetts. Many people work to protect the ocean. Let's take a look at what they do:

⌃ **Marine biologists** are scientists who study the lives of sea creatures. They help the rest of us understand how to look after them. Some biologists work on ships sailing far out at sea. Others are based at marine sanctuaries.

## Oceanographers ⟩

are also scientists. They are interested in the way the ocean behaves. Oceanographers record the temperature and saltiness of the waters around the world. They also make maps of the ocean currents that flow across the globe. The maps are useful for trade routes and for tracking ocean garbage. Some oceanographers use the latest submersibles (small submarines — see picture above) to dive deep into the ocean and study the seafloor.

## Fishermen

Most of the people who work in the ocean are fishermen. They have an important job in looking after sea creatures. Responsible fishermen use nets designed to trap larger, older fish but allow smaller, younger ones to get away. The young fish left behind can breed and produce more fish to catch another day.

# Words to Know

**Bacteria** Tiny, single-celled living things that exist everywhere and that can either be useful or harmful.

**Blubber** The layer of fat under the skin of a whale, seal, or other large marine mammal. It prevents the animal from freezing in colder seasons.

**Crustacean** A type of sea creature that has an outer skeleton and limbs that it uses for swimming or crawling. Crustaceans include crabs, lobsters, and shrimp.

**Current** The movement of water in a definite direction in the ocean.

**Mammal** A warm-blooded animal that often has hair or fur and usually gives birth to live babies. Female mammals produce milk on which to feed their young.

**Mollusk** An animal with a soft body, no spine, and a hard shell that lives in water.

**Nutrient** A substance such as a protein, a mineral, or a vitamin that is needed by animals and plants to stay strong and healthy.

**Plankton** Tiny animals and plants that drift or float around in the ocean.

**Prey** An animal that is hunted by another animal for food.

**Reptile** A cold-blooded animal that slithers or crawls across the ground or creeps on short legs. Sea turtles, sea snakes, and marine iguanas can also swim.

**Scientist** A person who has studied some area of science and uses it in his or her work.

**Sensor** A part of an animal that can detect and measure changes in the environment and send that information to the brain.

**Tentacle** One of the long, flexible limbs of some animals, such as the octopus and squid. Tentacles are used for moving, feeling, and grasping.